The Less Than or Equal to Love

OrangeBooks Publication

1st Floor, Rajhans Arcade, Mall Road, Kohka, Bhilai, Chhattisgarh 490020
Website: **www.orangebooks.in**

First Edition, 2026

ISBN: 978-93-7426-223-8

Price: Rs. 300.00

Printed in India

The ≤ Love

TRVSS PAVAN RAJU

OrangeBooks Publication

www.orangebooks.in

"A Series of Quotes Representing Love"

What Lies Inside this Book?

To feel the essence of "Love," one must attain some experience. People try to find their love at various instances or build a connection which leaves a mark in their life. In this book author tries to picturize different ways a person can understand "Love" i.e... how we are connected to different persons, places, situations etc. With each Quote author tries to establish the same in his words.

This book is lovingly dedicated to the memory of my father, whose love and guidance continue to inspire me.

Contents

"Women"

It all starts with pain…
Will of Her's…
Unbreakable…
Womb that carries us…
Breaking all her pain…
Into smile of ours…
Safest place in the heaven…
Her greatest journey…
Starts as mother…
Smiles that she brings…
As a daughter…
Guards us like a sister…
Shares her life as life partner…
Every role that she plays perfectly…
Whichever side we are of Her's…
Only a women could do it…
As a mother, As a girl, As a wife, also as nobody…

Insights

In this quote the author tries to depict the greatness of every woman. The first woman that we come across is our mother.

She has gone through unbearable pain to bring us into this world. We can define her will as unbreakable.

Her journey starts as a mother with a tremendous pain to see a smile on our face. Secondly the author conveys the next important roles that a woman plays.

As a sister she always mentors you and ensures you that you are going in the right path.

As a wife, accepting you as a partner and standing by you in every situation and acting as a wall to protect you…

Whatever role any woman plays…

She will be a picturization of perfection…

Whichever side you are of her's…

This is what "Women" are...

As a mother, as a girl, as a wife, also as nobody…

To be Loved!!!

The first breath of Love…
And the day began…
With the warmth of her touch…
Eyes shredding tears…
Smiles spreading all across…
Pain that she had gone through…
Long waited were the Months…
Making her the strongest of them all…
My blurry eyes could feel her sense…
Outspoken were the words…
Words that I Murmur…
Only she could Comprehend them…
And the day began…
Where I took…
The first breath of Love…

Insights

Through this quote author tries to convey birth of our emotions which is portrayed by means of love of mother towards her newly born child. How a child sees the world initially through his/her mother's eyes. There lies the undefined language of love, and it is the strength of every living being lying in the hands of every mother.

***

Words We Speak of

Days pass by…
With "You" & "Me" Singing…
Notes of "Maa" & "Tha…" All along…
Months of transformations…
I took…
To see the glaze on your face…
Bringing endless smiles…
Just like a clap of your hands…
Crawling on your back…
Were the moments…
Depicting the effortless nights spent by you…
Making me stand still…
Days pass by…
With his & her joyous smile come by…

Insights

There is no language of love. Through this quote author tries to explain the bonding between a mother & baby communicating with each other. As time passes slowly baby starts to utter the word “Maa.” And that is the joyous moment that every mother waits for.

Try recollecting the moments with your mother…

Unfortunately, human mind doesn’t have the tendency to recollect those moments when they were as a baby…

Author’s intension here is to make you “visualize” those moments, which obviously one can do.

Hope those pictures that you visualize & capture in you now…

Let there be a long-lasting smile that you can see…

“Defining her love for you in her eyes…”

***

"Soul"

"Never a Soul took anything…
Along with it…
But I made my Soul…
To Console…
And took my feelings of Love…
Along with Me."

Insights

Here the author tries to represent his world of imagination.

There lies an endless loop of eternal love which he carries all along his journey.

As in the real world, the only thing he could ask for is "Her Love" and convinces his soul to carry "each beautiful moment that she was on his side."

Persons may come and go as we have a time bound life…

But these moments are the ones that the author wants to carry along with him once he leaves this world...

***

"Petals"

"Petals keep falling…

Oh, my love…

Time passes by…

Everything becomes dry and lifeless…

But…

Flame lit by a true Soul Never Vanishes…"

Insights

“Essence of love...
In my words...” #

In this quote the author tries to imagine human life to that of a flower. Over time, petals of flowers keep falling and on a certain day it becomes lifeless similar to aging in humans.

The only difference is the origins of the term “Love” are so deeply rooted that “flames” lit by true “soul” never vanishes away…

***

"Her Beautiful Eyes"

Cold were the mines…
Hot waves litting through in vain…
Clouds that hovered…
Were getting wet…
Waiting for darkness to Lustre…
Winds that blew across her eyelids…
Touching glazing mines…
Were always mine…
Cold were the mines…
Asking for the sun to shine…

Insights

"Vision of my love...

In her closed eyes..." #

Through this quote the author tries to convey his love in a very romantic manner, describing the real beauty lies in understanding the depths of his love conveyed in his lines.

"Cold were the mines…Hot waves litting through in vain…"

It means usually the mines are very hot & always there are hot waves that swirl across inside. But his love has the energy that he feels the warmth of her presence which makes him stone cold.

"Clouds that hovered…Were getting wet…Waiting for darkness to Lustre… Were always mine…"

It means that happiness seeing her makes tears about to flush out of my eyes, but they are only waiting for her slightest vision through winds that are blowing across her eyelids, increasing my heartbeats as if I were touching glazing mines… these are the moments that I am still dying to live for… were always mine.

"Cold were the mines… Asking for the sun to shine…"

Cold were the mines... in my imagination… Waiting for moments relentlessly to view the sun of my love shine in her eyes…

"The Sand"

With minutes coming down…
Moments passing by…
Fallen are the loved ones…
Sprouts sitting under the shades…
Feared are the rains of dust…
Saying storms are not gonna stop me…
Let the rest face their dust of luck…
Here I fight alone…
Holding tight for the wind of storm to cross…
Fallen are the loved ones…
Raised are the ones who stood by them…

Insights

Through this quote the author wants to convey his state of mind when he is confused about the survival of his love.

He points out the moments when he has just seen the sprouts of his

love growing…

There comes a rain of dust which is trying to pluck them out…

But still, they are standing facing their dust of luck...

Not all the sprouts could withstand the storm…

There comes a stage where the person we love is taken away…

Left are the others who love us and stand by us till our last breath…

***

"My Future"

Wings cutting of the edges…
With every edge of life…
Destined to fly…
Distances making no difference…
My thoughts are saying enough…
Making my world pry…
Hands showing apart…
With gates of the future being open…
Doesn't tend to mend are wings…
Wings cutting of the edges…
Waiting for the infinite ends to tie…

Insights

Through this quote the author wants to convey the importance of decision making. Here the author imagines himself as a bird flying in the air. Both wings represent the struggles that one must go through to make decisions in life. Supposing that there is no co-operation between his two wings. One of the wings tries to move left putting in all its efforts and the other wing tries to turn right with equal effort. And his body is withstanding the air flow. Sometimes we might be at the nearest gates of the world we imagine living in but destiny tears up apart because of the instantaneous decisions that we take. There comes a time in everyone's life that the choices we make led us to different paths. All that we can do is reset our mind and continue our journey that would make infinite ends tie and reach our goal one way or the other way around.

Imagine yourself standing in front of a door which opens for you to step into the world that you desire.

But both your hands are pointing in opposite direction, one to the left and another to the right.

Decisions…Paths…Destiny…Hope… might slow you down.

But…

Whatever you choose my dear… Move with utmost satisfaction…

And you will achieve whatever you desire...

A Smile on Her Face

Hearts gonna never din…
Kites gonna unlash…
Let's taste the sip of dreary life…
Said a beautiful turn…
Nonetheless...
Turning me into topsy turvy…
A turbulence that has been all along…
But…
There comes a smile on your face…
My sweetie better half…
That made all laws defy…
Sewing "Me" to a "Straight line…"
Holding "you" with turns all along…

Insights

Through this quote the author tries to convey how a smile on her face has the strength to change the way of his life.

Love filled in his heart for her shall never make an unpleasant sound…

Kites that were that were tied to the limitations of "Love" have been untied…

Let's together taste the sip of this unpleasant life…

Making my world upside down… confused but with you carrying me straight in your path of Love…

These are the moments when all his unpleasant notes that he heard and played before… were turned into music of Love…

With you holding me in all difficult moments all along…

***

"The Treadmill"

Clock is ticking…
Her wings looping me in an Ambush…
Clouds gonna hover…
With darkness lustred around…
Worlds of words we hear are Dumb...
Said the times of the past…
Not making you step aside the treadmill…
That's built out of your thoughts…
Step aside my dear…
Said the voice of "presence…"
Clock is ticking…
With your love of sun…
Glazed around me all along…

Insights

Through this quote the author wants to convey how blindly following other people's opinion may lead you to fall into a trap of life.

As human life is time bound journey…

With darkness glowing around…

You might not be able to listen and follow whatevcr every other person suggests you…

Imagining picture of their life through your eyes…

Is what, worlds would suggest you run after…

But there comes a voice of presence…

That will guard you and tell you that…

With you standing by your thoughts, will make your life shine

With brightness all along…

***

"The 3 Knots"

And the 90's had a start...
Born and grown in as if it were a minute…
It isn't the dawn…
Which I love... in this journey…
My dear…
With darkness all around…
Surging in your absence…
Lurking me into time-bound circles...
To and fro making me furious…
With infinite loops swirling…
Then came the enlightenment of love…
That cut all the loops with a grin…
It isn't the dawn…
Which I feared…
3 knots that represents a bond…
Any gusty winds that try to separate us…
Is what I fear…
Those I will be guarding you from…
24/7
Happy Marriage Anniversary My Love…

Insights

Born in early 90's. And the time passed as if it was a moment ago.

In her absence there was a lot of darkness that kept on growing and binding him into a timeless loop.

There came a smile on her face that changed his life.

3 knots that he tied during the marriage represented a bond.

Strong winds that try to separate them both is what he feared, and he will always be protecting her from them…

His love for her being 24/7 (Endless)…

***

A Ray of Hope

Everything seems to blink…
When all the smiles are diminished...
Will is killed like in the darkness of misfate…
Time’s let go our hands free…
All fingers pointing towards failure...
But there comes a light…
Brings a ray of hope…
Hope which might not bring you success…
But stands with you…
Until your illness gets cured…
Everything seems to blink…
When he is on your side…
You will feel your will…

Insights

Through this quote the author wants to describe one situation in his life where he has touched the bitterness of failure, and he was unable to accept the fact. With all hopes gone, it was a gentle friend who came as a light and added brightness to his path. Although not sure whether the path will lead to success or not but at least it helped the author to move further and get out of that situation and boosting his will to stay strong and move ahead in life further.

***

"Life"

Silence beat the echoes…
Long forbidden are the Noise...
Transformed by the struggles…

Beats aren't overheard for…
Such a feeble sour life…
Questioning your existence…

Here I stand in my Dreams…
To bring voice to them…

Silence beat the echoes…
With all stupid decisions to repent…
And there exits the line of liveliness…

Liveliness I thrive…
But can't afford…

Insights

Through this quote author wants to convey the aftermaths when a decision we took in the past haunts us and voice of repentance keep murmuring in our ears.

Only way to silence them is to recognize your struggles and start dreaming afresh. Once you recognize your efforts and try again from the beginning you might succeed.

In case of author, all those dreams he had were tarnished in this stage.

He failed again.

Yet, his thrive to win shall definitely taste him the sip of success…

***

"Staying Calm & Speaking to Your Inner Voice..."

There you reside…
My Dear…
Nonetheless…
Facts speak of words that I hear…
Are dreadful…
A belief that you exist with me…
My heart is filled with enlightenment…
An intangible feeling of Love💕…
Showered in pure bliss…
When it's time…
I will be purely yours…
What is that I fight for…
Empty handed…
Craving for others happiness…
Nothing is to lose or gain…
At your place…
Finally, I lost…
What is Mine…
My Dear…
Being yours forever…
In My Place…

Insights

Through this quote author wants to convey his stand for existence of his love.

People may continuously try to drag you down through tough words that they speak, trying their best to bring an impact on your thoughts.

There started a fight between me and my world.

It is then I recollect the fact that when my heart is filled with your love, love that makes me feel light from words spoken by others.

That directed me to the world of happiness, world that will be purely yours once we unite.

You were not for me then, but you taught me to fight with the world empty-handed.

There is nothing to lose or gain when you are in my heart which is the right place for you to reside.

Only thing that I lost in your place is my heart, being yours forever in my place.

***

"World of Mirrors"

Yeah…
I looked into my world of mirrors…
It did show me a bright side of my soul…
I started looking in it…
Hoping to find the other brighter side…

Hope!!!
What a childish hope…
Making me dig through…
Through opaque me…
All this time…

Unable to understand…
There are always shades…

When there is ray of hope in front…

Insights

Through this quote author wants to convey the message that there will always be up's and downs in one's life. Here author tells a situation where the author through his imagination peeped into the world of a person shown in his mirror.

There he could see the brighter side of his soul.

But false hope would lead to disasters sometimes.

So, there are two things that the author wants everyone to understand

1. It was only his imagination and there was no use in digging inside the feelings of a person inside the mirror. He needs to understand that his thoughts are much more transparent than the one stuck in the world of his imagination.

2. Whenever the brightness of your thoughts shine at you. There will always be shades of darkness that shall form. You need to withstand them and move ahead. As you step ahead there is always ray of hope in front looking for you.

***

"It's My Birthday"

Learnt were the words…

That ain't scribbled…

Dodged were the years…

Passing by were moments…

Held by tongs…

That measure my success & failure…

Over Years…

As of such…

Is my life spent & will be spent always…

I thank everyone whom I met & will meet…

Moments…

Each one…

Bearing their own weight in mine…

With years of life spent…

There begins a journey…

Silently…

Held by tongs…

Insights

Through this quote, author wants to convey that as we grow with time our past keeps on adding up memories with each day passing by. The context of referring to the word "birthday" here is that with each birthday we start our new steps ahead. In the current situation you might be in a very tough situation, but there will always be some hand that helps you in need. You might fail sometimes, post all your efforts. But it's "Time" that heals you and takes you through success.

In authors view "With years passing by" success and failure both are held by "tongs" that make life even and help in holding our "LIFE" with tough grip in a balanced manner.

He is very thankful to all the people who have supported him at every turn of his life.

***

"Wake Up Call"

Beneath the darkest shades…
Holds the thinnest breath…
Alluding to the new realms…
Where kings rule the heavens…
And heavens that still stoop and grudge…
Seeking for peace on earth…
That held down its breath holding…
It's heaven up…
Here's life to differentiate…
One who is holding up is earth…
Doesn't tend to bend down…
Are Mankind…

Beneath the darkest shades…
Lie the darkest days to end…

Insights

Through this quote author wants to explain that our mind's greatest enemy is "Comparison."

"Alluding to the new realms…" line refers to the word comparison.

Every human being is gifted with their own special capabilities. These are not just supernatural powers.

"And heavens that still stoop and grudge…

Seeking for pcace on earth"

These lines refer to stating that although we are content with what we have achieved in our life, when a special guest named "comparison" arrives at our doorstep we must not encourage it and let it in. But we all usually tend to get attracted to seeing others' lives and comparing it to ours.

"One who is holding up is earth…

Doesn't tend to bend down…

Are Mankind…"

Through these lines author wants to convey that "Mother Earth" is known for her "Patience and Tolerance" towards it's kids i.e. all living beings. But human beings are lost in the world of Comparison.

***

"I Am Engaged"

Long were my travel…
Time's the one…
Counting on my distance…
My early 30's…
Gazing at my steps…
And whispering…
Your journeys are half trodden…
Here is the time…
To let trampled paths cross…
A better half…
Holding your hand and…
Making your footprints…
Amalgamate with her own's…
Now that we are "Engaged…"
I thank you for becoming my better half love❤…
Let our journey begin with flowers of happiness…
All along…

Insights

Through this quote author wants to explain the sudden change that happens when any person is getting engaged.

As a bachelor, in anyone's life many people may come and go out of your world. Once you get engaged your paths cross with a very special person who will care for you and lay a road of happiness that you have long waited for.

New expectations are set, which you may or may not fulfill.

What can you probably give her on an engagement day.

Its not gold or diamonds or silver that she hopes for…

It's your stand of her love that you take for her is what matters…

***

Peace

Gifted are the birds…

That fly…

I see them…

Leaves that withstand the gales…

Not shredded…

I could hear them…

Invoked are my human senses…

That could speak…

Thunders that struck…

Gave me a message…

Aking me to stay dumb…

Here is a silence…

That brought me peace…

Here I am now…

Among the gifted one's…

Insights

##Words Unspoken

Through this quote author wants to convey state of mind one should have. To lead a peaceful life, one should stay calm and understand the situation from different perspectives.

We as humans cannot fly by nature.

Watching birds fly…

Hearing the voices of leaves withstanding the heavy winds…

My human senses made me realize the fact that…

Thunders that struck in my heart, conveyed me a message…

To calm down my heartbeat…

And hear to the voice of silence…

That finally made me understand…

Gifted are the birds…

That fly…

With my thoughts driven as one amongst them…

Mom

Born as one…
Connected as two…
After 9 months…
Still lies a bond…
Which binds path for eternal love…
Although separated…
Death alone defies us…
But what still lies undefied…
Is love…
That identifies…
We are common as ourselves…
Pure love…
Is certainly Mom's love…
Forever lasting…
And…
Immeasurable…

Insights

##Eternal Love

Through this quote author wants to convey connection that is established between a mother and her child before and after his/her birth.

A bond that just paves a path for selfless love.

Death might just be a word that might take away your physical existence mom…

But it's your love that gains and let heavens fall apart for…

The walls of immeasurable love…

That you built across…

Laid unaffected,

Lasting forever…

***

School

It's my first day…

At school…

Was turning down the pages of books…

Enjoying the fragrance of new pages…

Unread were the pages…

Only a few images captured still…

Within a fraction…

Were years of lessons learnt…

Memories can't be forgotten…

Hmm…

It's my first day…

At school…

Whichever day I wake up…

Insights

##Memories

Through this quote author wants you to remember your times of schooling as a kid. We all enjoyed the fragrance of fresh pages of book.

Days passing by, with new lessons learnt…

Waiting for the school bell to ring…

We could hear those days in our memories…

As though they were yesterday…

“It’s my first day…

At school…

Whichever day I wake up…”

Everyday ends with a new lesson learnt…

And it also paves the way for fresh memories…

***

Roses

Fragrance is not one that…
Rose owes…
Thorns aren't the one…
That rip them apart…
What it owns is…
Beauty…
That binds its blood in...
Red…
Making it a beautiful rose…
That drags all our heart…
All along…
A Happy Rose Day…
To all Roses…

Insights

##Rose

Through this quote author wants to convey the pain that a little heart bears walking through the path of thorns in order to step into a new world…

The pain that it undergoes…

Thorns are the ones that lay across…

Beauty that is defined in it by birth…

It's about a Rose (Love)…

That every heart is embedded to…

***

Wisdom

Words unspoken…

Memories eroded…

We gain…

We lose…

There is nothing we owe…

When we bid goodbye…

Body and soul tear apart,

Wisdom alone survives the battle…

Wise were the people…

Great were their stories…

Word's unspoken…

Memories eroded…

Insights

Through this quote the author wants to convey how powerful words are that every author tries to make understand through their writings in their own words. Years after they leave this world, they still give a clear picture of images of the world that they lived in.

As a newly born author, he wants to praise all the authors who have spread their knowledge over the decades through their books.

Wise were they to share their knowledge…

Through great stories of lessons learnt…

Words unspoken, memories eroded means…

Human memories are eroded once they leave their body…

Whatever is left unspoken. is silence…

Our body leaves our soul but…

Whatever the thoughts of wisdom that we share are left as a mark of knowledge that cannot be erased and will be of help to future generations…

“My standing ovation to all the writers who let their

Knowledge spread for generations through their books…”

Looking for a New Life

"At last, I was to the shore…
I feared to turn back…
As one of the tides…
Was trying to swallow me up…
All my ideas were drowned…
But a ray of hope…
Was making me stand still…
I was looking at the tides…
And saying…
"You made me ruin myself"
"I am now as I was never before…"
My gateway to the new life…
Is ready to open…"

Insights

“Hope” lets your life “Live…”

Through this quote the author wants to convey a stage where he had reached a point where he failed trying.

Something that ends has to find a place somewhere to begin.

Author somehow built courage and swam across the tides of his past that were trying to swallow him.

Now that his fear of repeating the same mistake is haunting him.

Whatever newly he tried, all those ideas were getting drowned.

Hope is really good friend of his…

He looked at the past and said, “although you made me ruin at one point of life” I am now as never before…

My steps towards new life have begun…

We do fail in achieving many goals…

Those failures should be remembered and our successful future that is waiting for us should turn back & smile at the tides (past) that once tried to swallow us.

The Past

There is no use in collecting torn pieces from the past…

What you have seen is Epilogue…

The unread/unwritten future is ahead…

Which is waiting for you…

That day when u read your life…

As a Book…

A smile strikes on your heart…

That moment is enough…

To prove your words…

To be a complete story…

Insights

As mentioned in earlier quote description, one has to get away from the past. You cannot say that you have enjoyed reading a book just by reading first or last pages. Try reading yourself as a book. Wait patiently. One day or the other a smile definitely strikes your heart.

That moment is enough…To prove your words…

To be a complcte story…

***

A Clown

"To get into a clown's heart…
Is to tear a drop of water into two…
Although we broke it into two…
Yet…
It makes no difference in…
Fulfilling our thirst…"

Insights

When we consume something, we can easily identify the taste of it.

For example, the soup is sour, water is salty, sugar is sweet etc....

“Love” doesn’t work that way for everyone…

Likewise, a clown tries to bring smiles into others’ lives through his act but ensures that the sourness in his life doesn’t spoil the food (i.e. entertainment that he is giving you via his act).

To put it in another aspect of life, we may not get in return what we love, but that doesn’t change the fact that we still have the same love in us. Such is purity, so is the love that author had for her. Being a clown in her heart, loving her forever, forgiving the fact that she was the one who broke his heart.

***

The Vision

Her eyes were blue…

Mine were red…

It's the world I imagine of…

Difficult to contrast…

Hard to Imagine…

Here I am with a Gifted Vision…

That doesn't blink…

Her eyes were blue…

Beautiful in my heart…

Insights

Here the author wants to convey about the world that he built in his eyes that carry love for her.

In his imagination, he is gifted with a vision that sees love in her eyes continuously without a blink of eye.

Her eyes were blue… Mine were red… Beautiful in my heart…

These lines express a feeling of joy knowing that he fell for her…

***

The Ink

Ink's been empty…

Left with blindfolded words…

Fingers swirling across air…

Getting ready to bound…

Words that I create…

Kept them unfolded…

Ink's been empty…

Words set aflight…

Insights

Here the author is in state of confusion. It's like when you are getting multiple ideas, but nothing is working out.

There will be a set of outcomes that you expect, but life has something else planned for you already.

We need to stay calm and wait until the ink of emptiness is erased.

***

Tears

Tears were tasty…
Tasted by tongue…
Lips that murmured…
Reaching heart…
Were unheard…
Crumpled voices that echoed…
Were beautiful were opaque…
What you hear is only a bluz…
Heard passing through…
My Heart…
Tears were tasty…
Tasted by tongue…

Insights

Here the author wants to convey that his feelings for her were hidden deep in his heart. Music of love inbound in him which echoed but were not transparent to her. The reason author mentioned tears were tasty is, human tongue is known for its self-healing capability, it can heal but the pain caused by her memories were tuff to erase.

***

A Chance

Chances were few…
Choices to make ahead…
Wavering thoughts…
Asking to take step aback…
Tempting mirages…
Seeking for thirst to fulfill…
Few were the men supportive…
Lead me through a path…
Undepictable…
But instinct…
Chances were few…
Taken along a rough path…

Insights

Mirages often mislead us thinking that there is water there.

Illusions that are created in the road of love make our thoughts waver, but our thirst for love makes us blind and drags us ahead.

Although the chances were very less and result being unpredictable, still there are few men who support and stand by us irrespective of its outcome.

***

The Wait

Wait is over…
Were saying the tides…
Hopes gone tarnished…
You are the one…
For whom…
The real wait is for…
Fate chuckled across…
Garnishing the memories…
I spent with you…
Late was I to realize…
I am the one…
Who's the scrumbling…
Wait is over…
Were saying the tides…

Insights

Here the author wants to convey the feeling that all wounds have to recover some day or the other. After prolonged waiting period, there still lies a hope that he might succeed in his love. It's the time when fate smiled and showed author a glimpse of memories that he spent with her. In those pictures, to his astonishment he could only see that all the knots of love through which he bound her in his circle of love had now been cut. Now as there is emptiness saying wait is over…

Move ahead… saying were the tides.

***

The Hand

Steps taken across the Paths…
That wounded me…
Hands that let go…
Finding them…
Difficult to cross…
There is a woman…
Holding my hand tight…
Tough is the time…
Get across holding my hand…
Love is un-definable…
Fate fails…
Tough are the mom's pains…
That took our pain across…

Insights

In tough times, I could see people leaving me abruptly, only when I needed them the most. There was only one woman that believed in me and held my hand tight and said, "You are facing a tough time Dear," just stay along with me and I won't let you deviate from your path of destiny. Her immeasurable love made my wounds heal. And there came a day when fate had to accept its failure realizing "tough were her pains" covered just to see a layer of protection to flee our pain away.

***

The Arrow

My mind is a bow…
Arrow is my heart…
Thread lies in you…
My Love…
Once we get tied…
With you on my side…
Hitting the right shot…
Isn't a tough target…

Insights

Here author wants to convey a level of confidence that builds across him when she is with him.

It's a bond of Love that he is trying to get tied to eternally…

"Once we get tied…With you on my side…Hitting the right shot…

Isn't a tough target…" means, once her love is on his side there is no force that could stop him from achieving success.

***

The Storm

"Heights" not to compare…
"Weights" not meant to be bothered…
Smiles those given were always forsaken…
Dust storms that blow across…
Too little to reach the eyes…
Slight were the tears…
That led through Her's…
Wiping away…
Dust Storms…
That blew across…

Insights

Through this quote author wants to convey how he placed a protective layer to her through his “love.” I won’t see the heights I can reach to safeguard her. No weight (situation) can bend me down. She might forget the smiles that I brought her.

Here “Dust of storms” refers to tough situations that would get nullified before reaching her. Slight were the tears that led through Her’s wiping away dust storms that blew across means “I am the reason of tears she has. She may feel it as pain for a second but those were only to remove the same tough situations that passed away gently, with me wiping away them all along.

***

Anger

Tightened Lips…
Persuade my anger…
Not to drain me…
Into its well…
All the glow…
That I possessed…
Shaded in a moment…
Moments to regret…

A five-letter word…
That took my heaven…
To hell…

Tightened Lips…
Persuade my anger…
Not to drain me…
Into its well…

Insights

Here the author wants to convey the aftermaths of "Anger."

Tightened lips means my lips are asking me to stay shut and they are not opening.

Persuade my anger means, in case I utter something wrong when I am in anger, it would sink me into its well.

Once our actions are done negatively in anger, we would certainly not get the same respect what we had before, because of the words we used. Only thing we can do is to regret it.

Five letter word is "ANGER" due to which we are dragged into hell. Importance of staying calm is always a better option when you are angry.

***

Critics

World's gonna criticize…
My dear…
People show you down…
It's not your turn…
Dominance wins…
Says ignorance…
They smile…
They praise…
World's gonna criticize…
My dear…
Do not bend down…

You are simply now…
What they are not worthy to become…
In their lifetime…

Insights

Here the author wants to convey that one needs to be unaffected by other people words. He should take "good" inside his head if possible and leave the negative words behind.

Always there will be someone in the world to criticize. They show you down. Let them dominate once, as if it is not your turn to act now. People praise and also make fun. Remember that you should never bend down, as you already know the fact that what you are now, they are not worthy of becoming in their entire lifetime.

***

The Crying Baby

Baby is crying…
Distant clattering…
Wakes sleeping one…
Her blur eyes…
Filled with Love…
Searching for Mom's slight touch…
Turning all cries into smiles…
Toys that waver her mind…
Very few kept as memory…
Her eyes searching for…
Everything that's new…
Baby is crying…

Only the old touch…
Could bring back her smiles…

Insights

Through this quote author wants to convey bond between mother and her child.

A baby gets awake hearing the loud noises nearby. She is not completely awake, and her blurry eyes search for her mother while the tears roll across her eyelids. Usually, we come across kids carrying away their thoughts for a moment if any new toy is kept near them. But it's the mom's gentle touch that could stop a crying baby and bring a smile on her face. It's the love of her smile that even the stone hearted ones could melt down and bow down to.

***

The Shade

La... La... La la lah…
Weren't these the breeze…
Passing underneath…
Years of shades…
That life had it on you…
Like the awning…
Gone are those moments…
It's offset time…
Bringing on some music of Enlightenment…
Back again…
Weren't these the breeze…
Passing underneath…
La... La... La la lah…

Insights

Time moves on swiftly…

As if it were a song…

With years passing like, you were under its cover…

With high's and low's in its notes…

Gone are the moments…

Change is what it brings with the music of enlightenment…

Time moves on smoothly my dear…

As if it were a beautiful song.

***

The Prayer Beads

Chains that bound their culture…
Knots tied around legs…
Birds that were set to fly…
Were found lying on grounds…
With knots broken…
These were the same prayer beads…
That I pray to God…
Storms that came in their lives…
Aren't that strong go break their will…
Oh Lord!!!
They have had a bad dream…
Let Love of daylight…
Shine across…

Insights

Through this quote author wants to convey his anger over getting abused. Being born in a culture where women are respected utmost. We still see some situations or people suppressing her voice.

“Prayer beads” are the most sacred things that help to build connection with God during prayer. Author gave the same respect to “women.”

He prayed to God to act and drag them away from those bad dreams and keep his shine of love upon them.

Before abusing any women in future, people should fear seeing strength of almighty always shining on her.

***

Her Smile

Sounds that we hear…
Designed were the machines…
To measure…
Smiles that I see in her eyes…
Wish there were devices…
That could measure…
All that I see now…
Is a dream…
Opened were my eyes…
Dreaming her love forever…

Insights

Here the author wants to know if the person he loves has same feelings for him. At this point of time, author has no courage to ask her directly if she loves him. So, he conveyed the same feelings via this quote.

Usually, we can measure the frequency of sound that we hear. But unfortunately, there are no devices that could measure the love of smile in her eyes. So, only in his dreams he could measure them. In reality she was the love of his eyes that dreamed for her forever.

***

Mom's Love

Mistakes that I make…
Life's gonna act harsh…
Everything seems to be losing…
Darkness looping around…
A bright smile on my face…
Comes only when…
You are on my side Mom…
With your hands on my forehead…
Me lying on your lap…
Gone are the world of worries…
Feels like you holding me like a baby boy…
With all the worries gone along…

Insights

Life's gonna treat you harsh whenever you make mistakes.

Results would keep you on losing side.

You might see all good ideas getting drowned and you finally lose.

In such tough situations you could see a hand on your forehead tapping gently and saying, "Calm down my Dear."

Finally, a smile comes to my face.

With me lying on your lap, I feel like all worries are gone.

You are holding me like a baby boy with all worries gone along.

***

The Notch

Memories that we keep…
Aren't the one we owe…
What we own in reality…
Are far gone…
With slightest notch…
Keeping us bind together…
At least for a moment…
Memories that we keep…
Far gone are the ends…
Seeking for looping ahead…

Insights

We all have dents in our life. It means we might have failed so many times before succeeding.

With slightest “Notch” keeping us bind together means…

To make a structure, some edges need to be cut and joined.

We don’t carry the cut portions; we only go ahead with the structure.

Similarly, we need to throw few bad memories and concentrate on good ones in our life and move on.

***

A Friend

The word "different…"
Could only be found in his "Love…"
My Darling Friend…
You are mine…
However different we are!!!
We gain together…
We Lose together…
Angels that brought you in my life…
Are the ones…
That your heart owns…

Happy Friendship Day "MY LOVE…"

Insights

There is always one person in everyone's life.

He/She acts as an angel in your life.

You might have differences, but he/she never leaves you…

Whether you lose or win…

Heart that carries the purity…

Is what you own my dear friend…

Wishing you a happy friendship day.

***

The Scar

Beauty lies in Art…
We are all born…
With heart that beats the same…
Art is what you define…
Every definition that origins…
Has a scar that leaves us apart…

Knots that bind us…
Is there a touch of love…
Beauty tears us apart…

Formed are the shapes…
Of voices made through a Dumb Heart…
Beauty lies in Art…

Insights

We all are born with the heart that beats the same, which means…

At the beginning we carry the same amount of love. As time passes, the picturization of love is the one that varies. Scars that rip is apart are the ones that remain. But real beauty is that voices made through our dumb hearts are still knit by touch of love. That's where the "art" in us originates, each story echoing with different beat of love.

This is where the story begins…

***

Battle of Love

Born are the one's…
Who achieve…
Lost were the battles…
Which became history…
Souls that lost…
In this soil…
Aren't the lost one's…
True were their stories…
Praised only after they ended…
Ours is a battle…
Yet to end…
Doesn't matter…
I lose or I win…
I play on your side…

Either as loser or as a winner…

Insights

We remember the lost ones with their stories of achievement.

Souls that are lost in this soil would replenish.

True were their stories of Love.

My story begins with you and ends with you.

I will always be there for you.

This is what the author wants to convey.

When it comes to his part of the story, he might be a loser or a winner…

But he would always play on her side.

***

The Bond

Kites that fly…
Winds that blew…
Wavers its direction…
Here am I holding you…
Rolling on with one hand…
The other holding you and releasing…
Whichever way you like to go…
Hands that cut with slightest touch…
Wouldn't leave you…
Until you cut yourself up…
Kites that fly with a smile…
Staying united…
Setting you free…

Insights

Through this quote author wants to convey strength of his “Love” by taking “Kite” as an example.

Kites fly along with the winds that blow. They change their direction.

My love for you acts like a thread, roller tied to a kite. I hold you but letting you fly in whichever direction you move based on the winds.

I might get hurt (get cut) while holding the thread of our love, but I wouldn’t leave you until you cut yourself up (Until you set yourself apart from me willingly).

I see you flying with a smile, staying united, setting you free.

Author respects her whatever choice she makes.

***

Fear

World defined Donkey…
A lazy animal…
Lion as king of forest…

Reality is like…
You only fear when lion faces you…
Which will never happen…
If you constrain yourself…
Whole your life…

Lion will attack you and eat you…

It's that simple…
If you believe so…
That's gonna happen my dear…

Insights

Through this quote author wants to convey a simple message to move ahead in life and succeed i.e.

Believe yourself and never let fear of failure consume you.

***

The Lesson

Things that we learn…
Some taught to us…
Some learnt through experiences…
People we meet…
Some stay…Some leave…
Lessons learnt with or without…
A slap on your face…

It's who you are…
Whether world accepts you or not…
Whatever you are…
Stay as you are…
Till your last breath…
It's who you are…
Till the death defies you…
Portraying…
Who really you are…

Insights

Some things are learnt through teaching & some through our experience.

People we meet might stay or leave.

Life might teach you tough lessons with or without a slap on your face.

Author wants you to “stay” as you are.

Some day or the other they are going to know who you really are and start respecting you.

That day you might not exist in this world.

So, be you and be proud of what you have become.

***

Tides of Time

We seek for enlightenment...
Throughout our life...
When the path of truth...
Shines on us...
We become so blind...
We only see the darkness...
Which actually is brightness...
That we had trust to seek...
From years...
We are now incapable of seeking...
Only because the tides of time...
Blew us blind...

Insights

Imagine if someone just puts a flashlight directly on your eyes, you just come across darkness for a second.

Similarly, when the path of “truth” shines on us, we might become blind and see only darkness for a moment. But, believing that the darkness would be permanent, we begin to lose the trust that we had built from years of hard work.

These are tides of time that blew us blind.

You need to understand there are always good times ahead, just don’t stop believing in you, as your bright future is waiting just a step ahead if you are willing to move ahead.

***

The Colour of Love

Webs created...
Are the ones formed ...
One to protect...
Another to feed on...
Colours that keep changing...
In me...
Are the ones that chameleon does...

Formed are the colours that you love...
Every colour that I add on...
Is for you my love...

Lost is your vision...
Lost is my love...
Wherever you are...
Let ocean of my love...
Fill your life with the colours...
That I keep dwelling with...

Insights

A spider builds web. One is to protect itself from its enemies and another is to survive (for its own food).

A chameleon changes its colours, and So do I for you.

“Every colour that I add on is for you my love” refers to how author keeps on adjusting or transforming him as per her desires.

When she betrayed him, author says that she had lost her vision of his love and so is his love lost.

He wishes her that wherever she is, let the ocean of love that he carried in his heart fill her life with colours.

Left were the memories that author kept dwelling with rest of his life…

***

About Me

"I"

I ain't the art…
That portrays the Mind…
I ain't the speech…
That depicts the Thought…
I ain't the Skill…
That undermines me…
What's Unbounded is…
Slits ain't the one that I care for…
Will is what I am…

Insights

An artist always tries to picturize whatever he has in mind.

Usually, one's thoughts are transformed into speech.

A person is analyzed by the skill he has…

which is limited to one extent.

But here the author tries to convey that if one has willpower,

He can achieve anything at any point of time.

***

Ageless love

"Miles of journey taken across...
Defined were the paths of destiny...
Yet here I am at the tip of the Arch…
With thoughts trembling…
Mind wavering all along…
Such is life My Dear…
Wise were the ones who stood by…
Learnt aren't the lessons of "Love…"
Difficult to explain…
Only meant to experience the joy…
Miles of journeys taken across...
With frames of "Love…"
Dissipating all Moments…
As if it were a Snapshot…"

Insights

Here the author tries to point out his experience of "Love" as eternal light that flows through various stages of a person's life. There will be situations where things fall apart & destiny tests us. However, each step that one takes

turns out to be an unexplainable joyous moment. It is not about losing or winning the race of "Love." It is about memories that one carries in his life weighing as frames of his journey all along.

***

An Undelivered Note

The boy on the bike…
Holding his father with both his arms tight…
Carrying bundle of emotions…
Buckled up on his back…

His eyes seeing the world of fear…
That look can melt down your heart…
It’s on my way to school…
Said the boy…
When it gets nearer…
Boggled up were he…

These were the gates of knowledge…
Peeping to let you in…
This is the only time my father’s arms felt light…
Tensed were I to let go…
Never felt the same day would come in my life twice…

Moments that you left me alone today…
I am left at a new gate…
Standing there were you as always…
It’s only that I can’t feel the warmth of your weight…

Missing you dad…

Insights

Throughout his journey there was one person who constantly gave support to the author which is his "Dad." The author has shown his work of "quotes" to his father, he liked the quotes and was very proud of his son's work. Out of eagerness his father had asked him when he would be writing a quote describing him for which the author nodded gently with a smile. He didn't know what would happen next. Throughout his book author never got a chance to dedicate a quote to his father.

Author only completed half of the quote on his dad hoping that he would complete it next day & surprise him. Unfortunately, before the author could deliver the quote his father passed away. This is the reason why author has kept the name of the quote as "An Undelivered Note."

Coming to the explanation of the quote, it describes a boy who was on bike holding his father with both arms tight. He had lots of emotions buckled up on his back. They were on the way towards his school. His eyes that saw the world of fear thinking what will happen next when his father leaves him.

When they were approaching the school gate, he was getting overwhelmed or confused. These were the gates of knowledge that asked the boy to come inside. This was the only time when his father brought gently down his arms and let go of him.

Author never thought that he had to face the same day again in his life.

On his dad's demise, author felt like standing alone at a new gate.

His dad was standing with him as always, but the sad part is that author couldn't feel the warmth of his dad's touch.

***

My thoughts may seem blur to you…

What I say is…

Wear the glass of "Love…"

&

Enjoy the beauty of…

Every thought that I have…

Thank You

Hope you enjoyed the Quotes

- TRVSS Pavan Raju

To be Continued…

The Next Journey on its way...

The Lost Luster

Squandered are the moments…
That I let you into mine…
Hopes gonna tarnish…
Letting you live your moments…
Mine are the ones that Live…
Burnt in my heart…
Visible in my smile…
Viable only to love of Her's…
Not mine…
Squandered are the moments…
That I let you into mine…

The Dust Storms

The ones that we protect…
Are the one whom we care for…
Criss cross were our paths…
Making us happy…
For a moment where we meet…
Although for a short span…
Life's where it brings us a new turn…
Craving paths through your memories…
Vanished like a dust storm…
Settled inside her calmness…
Exuded are my feelings…
Leaving only her footprints…
That could never be eroded…
Though I am a sand of dust…
For Her's…
Lively from distance…
Fake is what you believe…
When you get close enough…

The Flair of Love

And the journey began…
Turns and twists…
Aren't the one I lay apart…
Timps that made you…
Music of my love…
My dear…
Are the one my heart carries…
All along…
Beats that go by…
Faster the one I own…
Making me Un-dying…
Now life's that big…
It's a flair of your love…
That echoes all along…

The Winds

Dwindling across the pines…
Shivers are the one left for…

Screeches are the voices…
Left far behind…

Freezing were the moments…
Of echoes that lay sting…

Here I come…
Signing…
Through the sigh of relentless efforts…
Winds aren't bending my heart beats any further…

Dwindling across the pines…

A Sister's Love

Roads been rough dear…
Here I am…
Holding my little fingers…

Sands of time slipping through…
Seeking for a hand…

Here comes an Angel…
That made me smile…
Through tough paths…
Smiles blossoming as a song…

"Who said Mother is the only Angel…
God's been busy all along…
Craving the body of another Angel…"

Here I am…
Standing in a path blooming…
Till the journey of sky…

I bow you my dear lovely Angel Sister…
For holding on my hand…
Here I am…
Paving my journey of Success…

Thoughts Never Say Goodbye…

Crazy dreams of life that I see…
Are gonna abruptly end…
To a sound of an alarm…
Which brings me into my world…
A world that runs out of time…
If I were slow to act upon…

With blurry eyes starts each day…
Thoughts wavering but…
Me sticking on to a routine…
That I wish I could skip…

My actions aren't gonna let me pass over…
Each day questioning my existence…

Here I am compelling my life…
To stay off the unrealistic dreams…
Striving to build an empire…
That lets me live…
Until…

Crazy dreams of life that I see…
Are gonna abruptly end…
To a sound of an alarm…
Which would take me away…
From this world…
Tend to end on a happy note…